ALL!GATORS

MELISSA GISH

PREDATORS X BOOKS

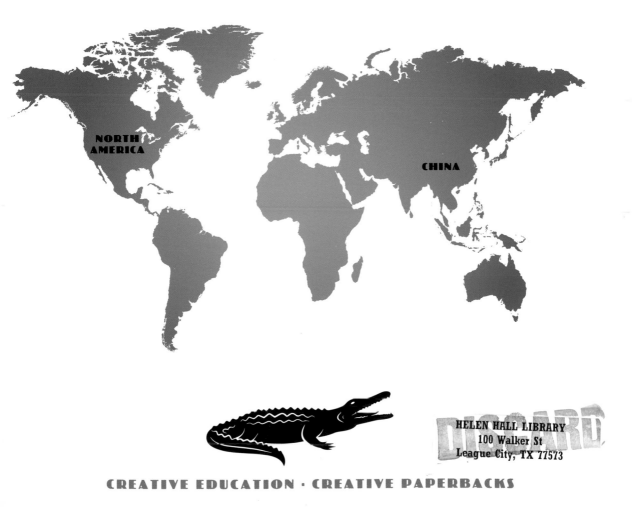

NORTH
AMERICA

CHINA

CREATIVE EDUCATION · CREATIVE PAPERBACKS

ALLIG

Published by Creative Education and Creative Paperbacks · P.O. Box 227, Mankato, Minnesota 56002 · Creative Education and Creative Paperbacks are imprints of The Creative Company · www.thecreativecompany.us · Design by Rita Marshall · Production by Chelsey Luther · Printed in the United States of America · Photographs by Alamy (Mark Conlin, Nature Picture Library, Doug Perrine), Dreamstime (Bugtiger, Eastmanphoto, Anton Starikov, Christopher Jimenez Nature Photo, yodke67, zobeedy), Getty Images (Ingo Arndt/Nature Picture Library, Henry Ausloos, TORSTEN BLACKWOOD, markrhiggins), iStockphoto (DianaLundin, Sergey Lavrentev, Elliotte Rusty Harold, Robert Eastman, pppdpl991), National Geographic Creative (KLAUS NIGGE), Shutterstock (Myrna Watanabe), FreeVectorMaps.com

· Library of Congress Cataloging-in-Publication Data · Names: Gish, Melissa, author. · Title: Alligators / Melissa Gish. Series: X-Books: Predators. · Includes bibliographical references and index. Summary: A countdown of five of the most dangerous alligator encounters provides thrills as readers learn about the biological, social, and hunting characteristics of these swamp-dwelling predators. Identifiers: LCCN 2016043696 · ISBN 978-1-60818-817-8 (hardcover) / ISBN 978-1-62832-420-4 (pbk) / ISBN 978-1-56660-865-7 (eBook) · Subjects: LCSH: 1. Alligators—Juvenile literature. 2. Dangerous reptiles—Juvenile literature. · Classification: LCC QL666.C925 G55 2017 / DDC 597.98/4—dc23 · CCSS: RI.3.1-8; RI.4.1-5, 7; RI.5.1-3, 8; RI.6.1-2, 4, 7; RH.6-8.3-8 First Edition HC 9 8 7 6 5 4 3 2 1 · First Edition PBK 9 8 7 6 5 4 3 2 1

ATORS

CONTENTS

Xciting
FACTS 28

Xceptional
REPTILES 5

Xtreme
TOP 5 ALLIGATORS

#5 **10**
#4 **16**
#3 **22**
#2 **26**
#1 **31**

Xasperating
CONFLICT 24

PREDATORS
X
BOOKS

Xtraordinary
LIFESTYLE 18

Xemplary
SKILLS 20

GLOSSARY

RESOURCES

INDEX 32

XCEPTIONAL REPTILES

Alligators are strong but patient. They watch silently. Then, in a flash of teeth, they strike. Their jaws are deadly. Alligators are extreme predators that rule North America's southern wetlands.

Alligator Basics

Alligators are **reptiles**. They are related to crocodiles. Alligators live in fresh water. Millions of alligators live in the southeastern United States. About 300 alligators live in China.

The bony ridges on alligators' bodies are called scutes. Alligators' green skin blends with the colors of their grassy habitat. This is called camouflage. Sometimes alligators float on the water like logs. Sometimes they sink underwater. Their ears and nostrils pinch shut to keep water out.

AMERICAN ALLIGATORS

American alligators live in swamps, rivers, and lakes in the southeastern U.S.

UNITED STATES

————— alligator territory

FEMALE AMERICAN ALLIGATORS

up to 10 feet (3 m) long; less

than 1,000 pounds (454 kg)

MALE AMERICAN ALLIGATORS

up to 15 feet (4.6 m) long;

up to 1,000 pounds (454 kg)

CHINESE ALLIGATORS

Chinese alligators are found only in a small area of China's Yangtze River.

CHINA

alligator territory

MALE CHINESE ALLIGATORS

about 5 feet (1.5 m) long;

about 90 pounds (40.8 kg)

FEMALE CHINESE ALLIGATORS

nearly 5 feet (1.5 m) long;

up to 90 pounds (40.8 kg)

An alligator's tail is about the same length as its body.

Alligators have webbed feet with sharp claws. To swim, they swish their long tails from side to side.

Alligators are strong swimmers. THEY SWIM FAST

Special flaps in the back of the mouth keep water out of the lungs. Clear eyelids protect the eyes.

Alligators are carnivores. They eat meat. Animals killed by predators are called prey. Alligators often hunt at dawn and dusk. Special **organs** on their jaws help alligators sense prey in the water. They can see well in dim light. They bite at anything that moves. Alligators have about 80 teeth. Their bite is one of the strongest of all animals'.

Alligators wait for prey to approach before striking.

ALLIGATORS ARE PATIENT

ALLIGATOR BASICS FACT

Alligators can hold their breath underwater for up to three hours.

TOP FIVE XTREME ALLIGATORS

Xtreme Alligator #5

Snorkeling Alone In June 2006, a man named Michael Diaz went snorkeling alone at Florida's Rock Springs State Reserve. Something hit his head. He thought it was a boat. But an alligator had grabbed his head. The alligator had a poor grip, so it let go. Michael pushed on the alligator's belly. It reached for him again. But Michael got away. He went to the hospital, where he got 33 stitches in his head.

Alligators normally shy away from humans. But they will bite anything that splashes near their heads—including human arms and legs.

Alligator Babies

A mother alligator lays 20 to 70 eggs. She buries them in a nest on land. After about 65 days, the eggs hatch. The baby alligators are called hatchlings. Without delay, they head for water. Sometimes their mother carries them in her mouth. Hatchlings are safer in the water. They can hide among tall grass and fallen trees.

Hatchlings already have sharp teeth and claws. They snatch floating insects and crayfish in their jaws. Small fish that come too close get chomped, too. With practice, the hatchlings will become fierce hunters.

Their mother protects them for about five months. After that, they stay near her for two years. But they must survive on their own. Four out of five will perish during this time. Within four years, they grow to nearly five feet (1.5 m) long. They are strong and fast. Their only fear is a bigger alligator.

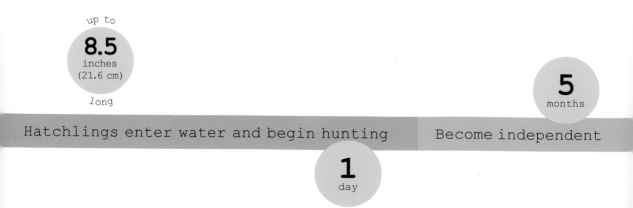

up to
8.5
inches
(21.6 cm)
long

5
months

Hatchlings enter water and begin hunting

Become independent

1
day

2
years

Leave mother

About 5 feet (1.5 m) long

7
years

9
years

Reproduce

4
years

ALLIGATOR BABIES FACT

If the temperature in a nest stays below 86 °F (30 °C), all the hatchlings will be female. If the temperature stays above 93 °F (34 °C), all the hatchlings will be male.

Xtreme Alligator #4

A Bad Hiding Place Late one night in November 2015, a man was sneaking around a Florida neighborhood. He had been breaking into homes to steal things. Some people saw him. They called 9-1-1. The police arrived. A helicopter searched for the man. He jumped into a pond to hide. The pond was a well-known alligator habitat. The thief was partially eaten by an 11-foot (3.4 m) alligator.

XTRAORDINARY
LIFESTYLE

Alligators are the top predators in the swamp. Young alligators share space with each other. Adults chase intruders away. Alligators control their habitats. Anything can become a meal.

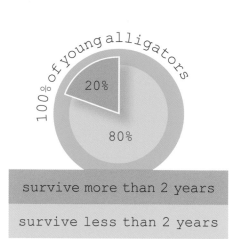

100% of young alligators

20%

80%

survive more than 2 years

survive less than 2 years

ALLIGATOR SOCIETY FACT

Alligators' tunnels can be up to 60 feet (18.3 m) long.

Alligator Society

Adult alligators do not like to share their homes. They establish **territories**. Females choose marshy places. Males choose areas of open water. They come together only to mate. This happens between April and July. They call to each other during this time. The deep rumbling sound they make is called a bellow.

Alligators dig pits in muddy ground. These pits are called gator holes. Each year they make their holes wider and deeper. Water collects in gator holes. This helps alligators survive periods of dry weather. Alligators also dig tunnels in the banks of rivers and lakes. At the end of the tunnel is a burrow. American alligators rest in their burrows for short periods in winter. Chinese alligators sleep soundly from October to March every year.

XEMPLARY SKILLS

Alligators can jump straight out of the water by pushing with their tails. They have even been known to climb trees and fences to get at prey.

XEMPLARY SKILLS FACT

Alligators can swim long distances at 20 miles (32.2 km) per hour.

The largest alligator ever measured was in Alabama in 2014. It was 15.75 feet (4.8 m) long and weighed 1,011.5 pounds (459 kg).

Alligators eat fish. They also eat small, furry animals called nutria. Nutria weigh up to 22 pounds (10 kg). They look like big rats. But alligators will eat anything they can catch. They even attack large animals such as deer.

Alligators do not chew their food. They swallow it whole. So they have a special way of eating large prey. First, prey is dragged into the water. With its prey in its jaws, an alligator flips upside down. It spins over and over many times. This twists the prey. The prey's body breaks.

3

TOP FIVE XTREME ALLIGATORS

Xtreme Alligator #3

Ignoring the Signs In the summer of 2015, a man was out with friends at a marina in southeastern Texas. Signs were posted warning of alligators in the water. People knew it was dangerous. But the man remarked that he wasn't afraid of alligators. Then he jumped into the water. Instantly, an 11-foot (3.4 m) alligator grabbed him. A friend jumped in and tried to help the man. She could not save him.

XASPERATING CONFLICT

Alligators normally stay away from humans. But sometimes they can't get away. Humans build towns and homes near lakes and rivers where alligators live.

Alligator Survival

Young alligators rarely attack people. But alligators more than five feet (1.5 m) long can be dangerous to humans. Alligators can leap five feet (1.5 m) from the water onto shore to grab prey.

Wildlife officers often remove alligators from places where people live. Thousands of alligators are caught each year. Some are taken to swamps away from people. Some are too dangerous to release. They must be killed.

Sometimes alligator populations are affected by other animals. Burmese pythons in Florida eat the same small animals that alligators do. They also eat young alligators. Wildlife officers try to kill these snakes. But they are hard to find.

ALLIGATOR LIFESPAN

Wild	about 50 years
Captive	more than 80 years ⟶

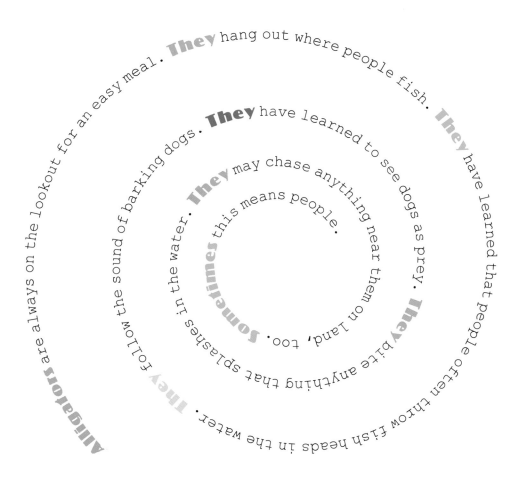

Alligators are always on the lookout for an easy meal. They hang out where people fish. They have learned to see dogs as prey. They have learned that people often throw fish heads in the water. They follow the sound of barking dogs. They may chase anything near them on land, too. They bite anything that splashes in the water. Sometimes this means people.

2

Xtreme Alligator #2

Climbing the Fence In 2007, two men were breaking into cars at a resort in Miami. Next to the resort was a retention pond. These ponds are used to catch rainwater. They have high fences around them to control flooding. Police searched for the men. One of the thieves climbed over the fence. He landed in the pond and met a nine-foot (2.7 m) alligator. He did not make it out alive.

Alligators can run short distances at up to 11 miles (17.7) per hour

Alligators are ready to mate when they are about six feet (1.8 m) long.

Hatchlings that are 8.5 inches (21.6 cm) long fit inside
eggs that are 3 inches (7.6 cm) long.

Alligators care for their gator holes year round.
They clear away mud and weeds.

A healthy alligator can survive two years without eating.

Alligators perform what is called a death roll underwater
to drown larger prey animals.

Alligators can hear each other's bellows up to 165 yards (151 m) away.

Alligators hiss when they are angry or defending their home.

Broken teeth are replaced. An alligator can
grow 2,000 teeth in its lifetime.

Alligators warm up in the sun. They go in the water to cool down.

Alligator mates blow bubbles in the
water with their nostrils as a greeting.

Young alligators can eat nearly a quarter
of their body weight in one meal.

Alligators slap their jaws together with a loud pop to communicate.

Alligator stomach juices are

strong enough to turn bone into mush.

Xtreme Alligator #1

Do Not Tease the Gators In 1985, a man and his friend went fishing in a Florida **canal**. They took their children. They saw three small alligators. One man decided to tease the alligators. He jumped out of the boat and punched one of the alligators. It wasn't so small after all. It pulled him under the water. His friend and children looked for him. They could not find him. His body was found two days later.

GLOSSARY

canal – a man-made waterway

organs – parts of a living being that perform specific tasks in the body

reptiles – animals with dry, scaly skin whose body temperatures change with their surroundings

territories – areas owned or claimed and defended from intruders

webbed – connected by a web of skin

RESOURCES

"American Alligator (*Alligator mississippiensis*)." University of Georgia: Savannah River Ecology Laboratory. http://srelherp.uga.edu/alligators/allmis.htm.

Howell, Catherine Herbert. *National Geographic Pocket Guide to Reptiles and Amphibians of North America*. Washington, D.C.: National Geographic, 2015.

"Kids—Learn About Alligators." Florida Fish and Wildlife Conservation Commission. http://myfwc.com/wildlifehabitats/managed/alligator/education.

Ouchley, Kelby. *American Alligator: Ancient Predator in the Modern World*. Gainesville: University of Florida, 2013.

INDEX

American alligators 5, 6, 19, 20

Chinese alligators 5, 7, 19

communication 19, 28

habitats 5, 6, 7, 16, 18, 19, 24, 26

hatchlings 12, 14, 28

infamous alligators 10, 16, 22, 26, 31

physical features 5, 7, 8, 12, 20, 25, 28

prey 8, 9, 12, 20, 21, 24, 25, 28

sizes 6, 7, 12, 13, 16, 20, 22, 26, 28

speed 20, 28

swimming 8, 9, 20

wildlife officers 24

Hatchlings call to their mother with unique croaking sounds.